W9-CCC-700

My New Home
After Syria

CRABTREE
PUBLISHING COMPANY
WWW.CRABTREEBOOKS.COM

Linda Barghoorn

CRABTREE
PUBLISHING COMPANY
WWW.CRABTREEBOOKS.COM

Author: Linda Barghoorn

Editors: Sarah Eason, Harriet McGregor, and Janine Deschenes

Proofreader and indexer: Wendy Scavuzzo

Editorial director: Kathy Middleton

Design: Paul Myerscough and Jessica Moon

Cover design: Samara Parent

Photo research: Rachel Blount

Production coordinator and
    Prepress technician: Ken Wright

Print coordinator: Katherine Berti

Consultants: Hawa Sabriye and HaEun Kim, Centre for Refugee Studies,
York University

Produced for Crabtree Publishing Company by Calcium Creative

Publisher's Note: The story presented in this book is a fictional account
based on extensive research of real-life accounts by refugees, with the aim
of reflecting the true experience of refugee children and their families.

Photo Credits:
t=Top, c=Center, b=Bottom, l= Left, r=Right

Inside: Jessica Moon: p. 29b; Shutterstock: 3D Creation: p. 4cr; Alexandr
III: p. 16b; AndriyA: p. 21b; AngelinaKo: p. 27b; Answer5: p. 18b; Brothers
Good: p. 6cl; CharacterFamily: p. 12bl; Nicolas Economou: p. 9l; Elbud: p.
24br; Elenabsl: p. 18t; Carlo Falk: pp. 6–7c; Jesus Fernandez:
p. 28b; Frank A: pp. 14–15t; Frank Gaertner: p. 23c; Great Vector Elements:
p. 23t; Mitch Gunn: p. 13; Muhammatarming Hayimalee:
p. 4t; Jazzmany: pp. 14l, 22t; Jemastock: p. 10br; Kafeinkolik: p. 7b; Helga
Khorimarko: pp. 18bl, 19t; Lemberg Vector studio: p. 16t; MidoSemsem: p.
26c; Monkey Business Images: p. 20c; Mspoint: p. 28t; Christian Mueller:
p. 23b; ONYXprj: p. 20t; Panda Vector: p. 12t; Procyk Radek:
pp. 8–9t, 24bl; Rkl Foto: p. 25; Robuart: pp. 24–25t; Sapann Design: p. 22b;
Smallcreative: p. 8b; Sudowoodo: p. 29t; Torgonskaya Tatiana: p. 12c; Eiko
Tsuchiya: p. 19; Venimo: p. 3; What's My Name: pp. 10t, 26b; Murat Irfan
Yalcin: p. 20b; Din Mohd Yaman: p. 5t; Zurijeta: p. 16c; UNHCR:
© UNHCR/Aubrey Wade: p. 27bl; © UNHCR/Gordon Welters: pp. 10bl,
11, 17c, 18–19t, 21c, 27t; © UNHCR/Gerhard Westrich: p. 15c.

Cover: Shutterstock: Jesus Fernandez.

Library and Archives Canada Cataloguing in Publication

Barghoorn, Linda, author
    My new home after Syria / Linda Barghoorn.

(Leaving my homeland : after the journey)
Includes index.
Issued in print and electronic formats.
ISBN 978-0-7787-4983-7 (hardcover).--ISBN 978-0-7787-4989-9 (softcover)
ISBN 978-1-4271-2125-7 (HTML)

    1. Refugees--Syria--Juvenile literature. 2. Refugees--Germany--
Juvenile literature. 3. Refugee children--Syria--Juvenile literature.
4. Refugee children--Germany--Juvenile literature. 5. Refugees--Social
conditions--Juvenile literature. 6. Refugees--Germany--Social
conditions--Juvenile literature. 7. Syria--Social conditions--Juvenile
literature. 8. Boat people--Syria--Juvenile literature. 9. Boat people--
Germany--Juvenile literature. I. Title.

HV640.5.S97B37 2018   j305.9'069140956910943   C2018-903015-1
                                                          C2018-903016-X

Library of Congress Cataloging-in-Publication Data

Names: Barghoorn, Linda, author.
Title: My new home after Syria / Linda Barghoorn.
Description: New York, New York : Crabtree Publishing, 2018. |
    Series: Leaving my homeland : after the journey | Includes index.
Identifiers: LCCN 2018029945 (print) | LCCN 2018032287 (ebook) |
    ISBN 9781427121257 (Electronic) |
    ISBN 9780778749837 (hardcover) |
    ISBN 9780778749899 (pbk.)
Subjects: LCSH: Refugees--Syria--Juvenile literature. | Refugees--
    Germany--Juvenile literature. | Refugee children--Syria--Juvenile
    literature. | Refugee children--Germany--Juvenile literature. | Refugees-
    -Social conditions--Juvenile literature. | Syria--History--Civil War,
    2011---Juvenile literature. | Syria--Social conditions--Juvenile literature.
Classification: LCC HV640.5.S97 (ebook) |
    LCC HV640.5.S97 B37 2018 (print) | DDC 956.9104/231--dc23
LC record available at https://lccn.loc.gov/2018029945

Crabtree Publishing Company
www.crabtreebooks.com   1-800-387-7650

Printed in the U.S.A./092018/CG20180719

Published in Canada
Crabtree Publishing
616 Welland Ave.
St. Catharines, Ontario
L2M 5V6

Published in the United States
Crabtree Publishing
PMB 59051
350 Fifth Avenue, 59th Floor
New York, New York 10118

Published in the United Kingdom
Crabtree Publishing
Maritime House
Basin Road North, Hove
BN41 1WR

Published in Australia
Crabtree Publishing
3 Charles Street
Coburg North
VIC, 3058

What Is in This Book?

Roj's Story: Syria to Germany

Hello! My name is Roj. I was born in Syria. I lived there for a short time with my parents, baba (father) *and* mama (mother), *and my* tété (grandmother). *I have two older brothers, Mohammed and Ali, and a sister, Saja. Our family lived in Aleppo. It was the largest city in Syria.*

Syria's flag

Germany's flag

EUROPE

Syria is a country in the **Middle East**. It shares borders with Turkey, Iraq, Jordan, Israel, and Lebanon.

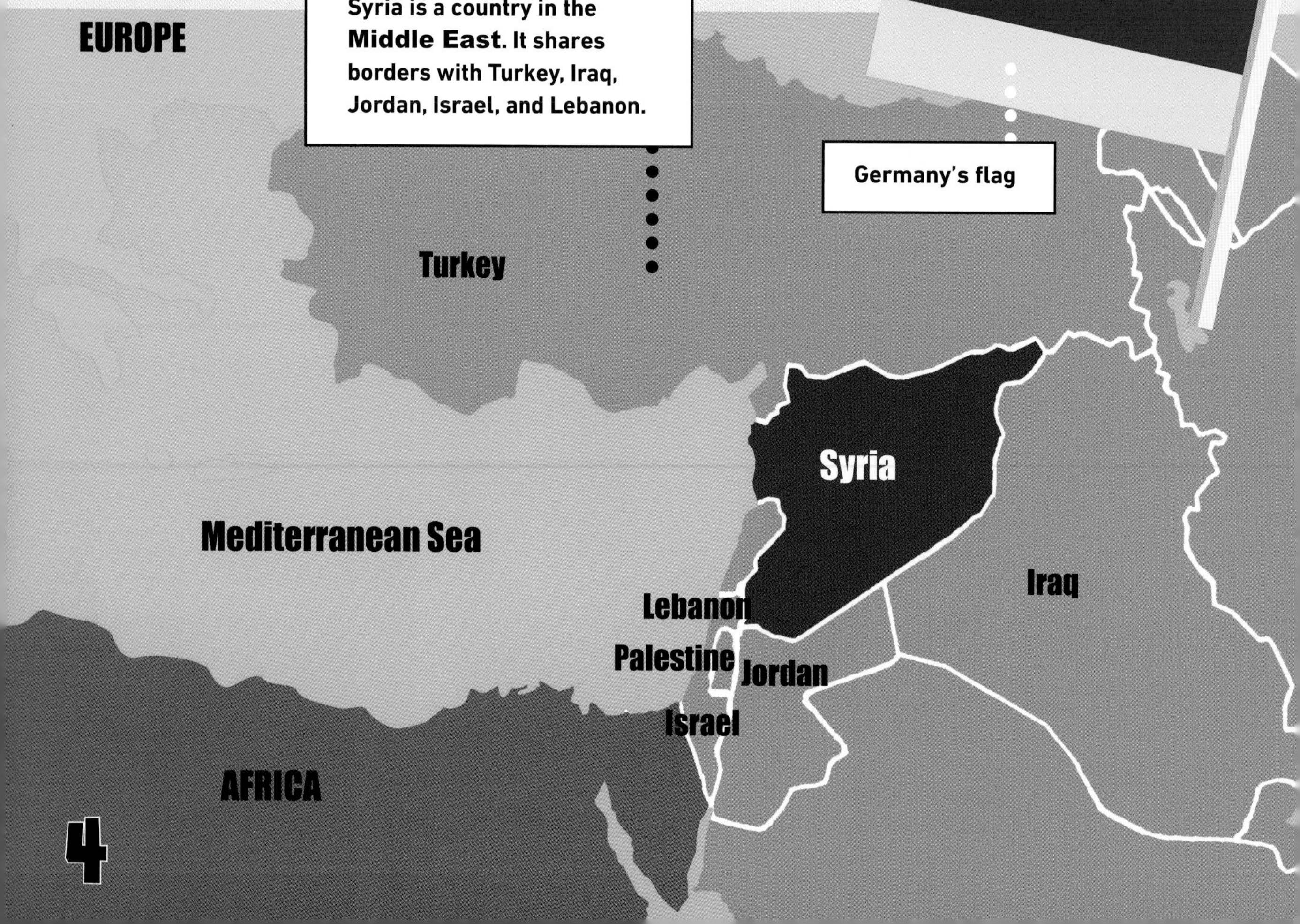

Turkey

Syria

Mediterranean Sea

Iraq

Lebanon

Palestine **Jordan**

Israel

AFRICA

Hundreds of thousands of Syrian children live in camps in neighboring countries. Many Syrian children lost their parents during the conflict, or fighting.

*I was 10 years old when we left our homeland. There is a terrible **civil war** in Syria. Many cities have been destroyed. Thousands of people have been killed. Many more have fled their homes. When the war came to Aleppo, my parents decided we needed to leave Syria. We are **refugees**.*

Now I live in Germany. We were given clean clothes, food, and a place to live. I am so happy to be safe with my family in Germany!

UN Rights of the Child

A child's family has the **responsibility** to help ensure their **rights** are protected and to help them learn to exercise their rights. Think about these rights as you read this book.

My Homeland, Syria

The Syrian civil war began because many people there were unhappy with how the government was run. They were not allowed to vote to decide who would be part of government. People **protested** in the streets. The government attacked the protesters, killing some and arresting others.

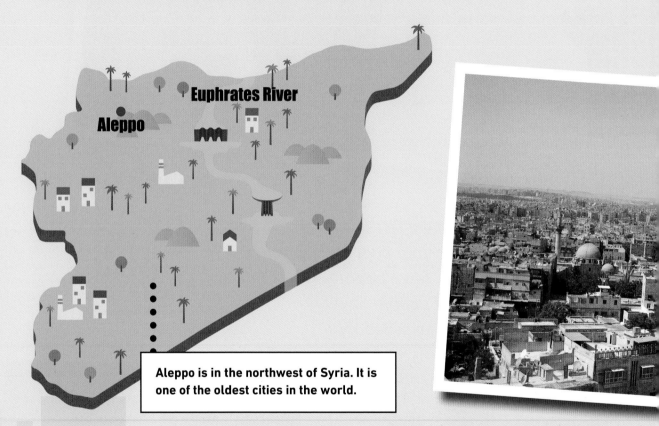

Euphrates River

Aleppo

Aleppo is in the northwest of Syria. It is one of the oldest cities in the world.

Today, there are many **rebel groups** fighting against the government. Each group wants to control Syria. Foreign countries are also involved. Some support the Syrian government. Others support the rebels. No one knows how to reach an agreement to end the war.

Syria is a beautiful and historic country. But much of it has now been destroyed. Millions of people have fled the country. Some have been granted **asylum** in new countries. Millions more have fled their homes but remain in Syria. They are internally displaced persons (IDPs). The war in Syria has created a **humanitarian crisis**.

Before the war, Aleppo was an impressive and beautiful city. Sadly, much of it has now been bombed.

Young Syrian children do not know a life without war. Those who are still in Syria are in danger every day. Food and safe drinking water are hard to find. Hospitals have been bombed. It is difficult to get proper medical care. Many schools have been closed or destroyed.

When the war started, many people were forced to flee, taking only what they could carry.

Roj's Story: Leaving My Homeland

It was hard for my parents to make the decision to leave Aleppo. We are proud Syrians. We enjoyed the wonderful food, art, and history of our country. Tété lived with us in Syria. She helped Mama make delicious meals for us each day. She tucked me into bed each night, too.

Refugee camps like this one provide **temporary** shelter for refugees. People live in simple tents there.

Many neighborhoods in Aleppo have been destroyed during the war.

When my school was bombed, Saja was badly injured. We were so afraid. Then Baba lost his job and a market near our home was bombed. My parents knew we had to leave Syria.

Story in Numbers

70 percent

of all Syrian refugees granted asylum in Europe have settled in Germany.

This makes Germany the number one destination for Syrian refugees in Europe.

We left and went to a refugee camp in Turkey. Then my parents paid **smugglers** to take us across the Mediterranean Sea to Europe. The boat was so crowded. It began to sink, and we almost drowned. My parents, brothers, and I were saved by rescue boats, but Saja disappeared.

We eventually got to Germany. And, one day, we received news that Saja was alive. That was the best day of my life! We found out that she had been pulled from the water by a rescue boat and taken to a different refugee shelter in Greece. People worked hard to find out if her family was alive. And, finally, they found us!

Many Syrian refugees travel across the Mediterranean Sea in small boats, packed with people. The journey is very dangerous.

A New Life

Refugees are forced to start over in a new country, often with few or no belongings. In Germany, the government provides refugees with temporary housing. It also gives the refugees some money to buy food, clothing, and other supplies. The government tries to get refugee children into school as quickly as possible. It also provides training programs and support to help adults get jobs.

Learning the new language and **culture** is important for refugees. It helps them feel part of their new country and allows them to fill out forms, take tests, and access services in the local language. Refugee children and adults receive language lessons. Children receive lessons for one year before they enter regular school.

Adult refugees in Germany must pass a test about German culture before they can look for work.

UN Rights of the Child

You have the right to live free from war. As a refugee, you have the right to special protection and help if you are forced to leave your homeland.

Many volunteer organizations have started up across Germany to help refugees. The Welcomegrooves Project offers German language lessons with a musical theme.

Volunteers often help refugees start new lives in their **host country**. They might help families find housing, look for work, and go shopping for new types of food. Or they might help with the paperwork needed to apply to a school or for a job.

Refugees also help one another. Many miss friends and families they left behind. Often they feel afraid and alone. By talking to other refugees about their experiences, they help support one another.

Roj's Story: Arriving in Altena

When we first arrived in Germany, a small crowd of people met us at the train station. They were clapping and waving. I did not understand what they were saying. But their big smiles made me feel as though everything would be ok. They gave my brothers and me backpacks. They were stuffed with clothes, shoes, books, and soaps.

Altena is a small town in Germany. Of the 400 refugees who have arrived in Altena, about 200 are from Syria.

For a while, we stayed in a shelter. There were many other refugee families there, too. We shared a room with another family. A bedsheet hung from the ceiling to separate our two families. But it was very noisy and crowded.

A volunteer named Harald visited each week to check on us. He helped us complete forms that would allow us to stay in Germany, help Baba apply for jobs, and let us go to school. Harald helped us find our way around the village where we live, and taught us how to ride the bus.

So much has changed since then. I have learned to speak German and I go to a German school. We live in a small apartment and Baba has found a job. Everything in Germany is so organized and clean because there is no war. The houses in our village have neat gardens and fresh flowers. I love it here.

Hi Bakr,
How are you? We have been in Germany for three months. The volunteers gave us new clothes when we arrived. My favorite is my new Bayern Munich football jersey. Maybe one day I will be a famous soccer player here. Ha, ha! I am making new friends, but I really miss you.
Roj

Maybe one day I'll play for Bayern Munich!

A New Home

At first, refugees in Germany live in shelters made in unused office buildings, warehouses, or schools. They can be crowded, noisy, and uncomfortable. Families may stay there for months or even years.

Life in these temporary homes is hard. Refugees do not have many chances to meet the local people. This makes it difficult to learn the language and get used to the local culture. Sometimes refugees face **racism** because they look and dress differently. They may feel unwanted in their new communities.

Sleeping areas in emergency shelters like this one are crowded. There is very little privacy.

Child refugees have lost their homes and toys. These are not things that can be quickly or easily replaced in a new country.

Housing is expensive and hard to find in Germany. The government is building more housing for the refugees, but it is not enough. Refugees must often compete with local Germans for the housing.

Refugees can find jobs as skilled laborers. This man is sewing cloth sails for ships.

Some refugees are sent to Germany's cities. But many are sent to smaller towns where they are more likely to find housing and jobs. Volunteers play a big role in helping refugees move out of temporary shelters. They help families look through advertisements for apartments, call building owners, and fill out forms. Volunteers may also drive refugees to see possible places to live.

Roj's Story: My New Home

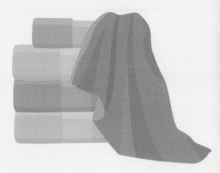

We lived in different shelters for more than two years. Then Baba found us an apartment. Now we live on the second floor of a building on the edge of town. Most of our furniture was given to us by a charity. Harald and some of his friends helped us move in. They even bought things for us such as bedsheets and bathroom towels.

Mama is happy she can cook meals in her own kitchen. But she misses Tété's help. There is so much packaging on food. We had to learn to recycle the packages so we do not create too much garbage. Each evening, our family eats and prays together. We sit on the worn carpet that reminds me of the one in our Aleppo apartment.

Meal times give families the chance to share the food, culture, and language of their homeland.

Our apartment building is in a row of houses and apartment blocks. Sometimes, I feel like our neighbors are watching us. Some are friendly and wave, but others look angry at us for living here. Every Saturday, we call Tété in Syria. We miss her so much. We worry about her because things in Syria are getting worse.

In Germany, it is common to use a bicycle to get around. This may be a new experience for child refugees.

Hi Tété! This is our new apartment in Altena. It is small. It sometimes feels crowded, but Baba says we should be grateful for our new home. I share a bedroom with Mohammed and Ali. Mama dreams of living in one of the little German houses with their neat gardens. I hope you be able to join us here one day. I miss you! Roj

A New School

Thousands of children in Syria have not been to school for years. Many schools have been destroyed in the war. Many more are empty because it is too dangerous for children to get there.

In Germany, young refugee children go straight into regular classrooms. Older children attend a one-year "welcome" class. There, they learn the German language and culture. Then they can move to a regular German classroom.

Teachers encourage refugee children to join in with their class activities as quickly as possible, so they get used to their new schools.

Students study a wide range of subjects in Germany. They might also participate in activities such as sports, theater, and music lessons outside of school.

You have the right to an education that allows you use and develop your unique talents and abilities, and that helps you learn to respect others.

Learning a new language can be challenging, especially when the alphabet is different!

peach خوخ

melon

apple تفاحة

After elementary school, there are different kinds of high school options. Some schools lead straight to jobs, such as a **carpenter** or an **electrician**. Other schools provide an education that allows the students to go to university.

The type of school children will attend depends on the grades they achieve by the time they are 10 years old. Refugee children are often behind in their education and must learn a new language at school. It can be very difficult to get a place at a high school that leads to university.

Roj's Story: My New School

I still remember my first day of school in Germany. Baba took me to school with Ali and Mohammed. We all had to attend the "welcome" classes. We could not speak German. My teacher smiled and spoke to me. I did not understand a word he said. At recess, I stayed in the corner of the playground watching the other boys play games. I felt lonely.

But now I speak German pretty well. I passed the language test and I am in a regular classroom with other German boys and girls. In Syria, boys and girls are in separate classes. My best friend, Dieter, smiled at me the first day I joined regular classes. He invited me to join a soccer game at recess. We have been friends ever since.

A new school in a new country can be a scary experience for refugee children starting new lives.

Story in Numbers

Only

1 in 100

Syrians understands or speaks German when they arrive.

May 4
I got a reply today from Bakr! I have been writing to him in the United States each month. He says that things are tough for them. They still do not have their green cards, which they need in order to stay in the US. He said the government has made new rules for Syrian refugees. They do not know what these rules mean. They are scared they will be forced to leave. I am really worried about him.

Learning and playing music at school can help refugee children express their feelings.

My brothers, sister, and I wake up very early to go to school. There are no school buses in Germany. Most students walk to school or take a public bus. Baba takes us to the bus stop. He catches another bus that takes him to work at a factory. We have lessons from 8 a.m. to 2 p.m. After school, Mama has lunch ready for us. Next, we do our homework. I am studying very hard. I hope to go to university one day.

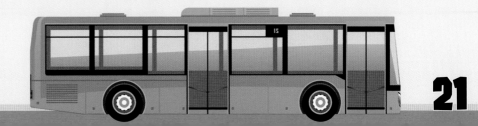

Everything Changes

Germany does not have enough people to fill all of the jobs available there. Refugees play an important role in filling these jobs. They also bring different ideas and traditions. This can **enrich** their local communities.

But some people in Germany are afraid of refugees. Often they are scared because the refugees are different in their dress, language, and religion. Some Germans believe that Germany has accepted too many refugees. These people worry that the refugees will take over their communities, jobs, and homes. Refugees often face **discrimination** from people who believe this.

Refugees worry about how they will fit in to the new culture. To help people understand this, Refugee Voices Tours shows people the city as though through the eyes of a refugee arriving in Berlin.

UN Rights of the Child

You have the right to practice your own language, culture, and religion, and to choose your own friends.

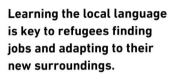

Learning the local language is key to refugees finding jobs and adapting to their new surroundings.

Not all refugees in Germany will be allowed to stay forever. Some have received temporary asylum. This means they must apply every year to extend their stay in Germany. They fear for their future because they do not know if they will be forced to leave.

Refugees want to feel that they belong. They want to contribute to their new community. Most also want to keep their own language and culture. It is important for them to stay connected to friends and family in their homeland. In Germany, local community centers, churches, and volunteer groups help refugees connect their old and new lives.

Being able to visit a **mosque** to pray can help **Muslim** refugees feel more at home.

Roj's Story: My New Way of Life

We still see Harald sometimes. Mama invites him to dinner to say "thank you" for everything he has done to help us. Harald says Mama's food is so delicious that she should open a restaurant. Mama no longer wears a **hijab**. She just wears a loose scarf over her head, which is also a Syrian tradition. Baba still works in the factory. He hopes to get a new job there to make more money. Mostly, we speak Arabic at home. But sometimes we practice German together.

These newcomers have found jobs at a local market selling fruit and vegetables.

These Syrian refugees in Turkey are wearing **burqas**. Refugees choose whether they want to wear a hijab, burqa, or no head covering in their host country.

There is no mosque nearby, so we do our morning and evening prayers at home. It is difficult to do our midday prayers because there is no time or place to do them at school. We are happy in Germany, but sometimes it can be lonely. German families are quite private. In Syria, we were always visiting with family and friends. Now we often spend evenings at home playing cards or studying. Dieter and I meet at each other's houses to do homework or play video games.

Bakr, How are you? Last month, one of Harald's friends gave us bicycles. We ride them to school and to weekend activities. Saja had to convince my parents to allow her to ride a bicycle. As you know, in Syria this is not what girls do! It was difficult with her artificial leg. But she was so proud when she learned to ride alone! Mohammed has almost finished high school now. He will soon look for a job. Sometimes, he fights with my parents. He wants more freedom to go out and be just like his new German friends. My parents worry he is not following our way of life, but it is hard to be both Syrian and German.
Roj

Everyone loves cycling in Germany!

Story in Numbers

In western Germany, **23 percent** of the population has some background as a refugee or **immigrant**.

Roj's Story: Looking to the Future

Baba's favorite German saying is "Alles gut." It means "everything is fine." Life can be difficult here at times. But Baba wants to show everyone that he is hopeful about our future here. Mama still dreams of returning to Syria. She wants to go back when the war is over. Then we could be with Tété. Mama and Baba have started a part-time catering business. Mama cooks delicious Syrian food for it. Harald helps them advertise in the local community.

UN Rights of the Child

You have the right to an identity—an official record of who you are—which no one can take away from you.

Syrian meals are made of many different dishes. They use a variety of vegetables, meats, and grains.

This learning center teaches computer skills to young refugee women.

Mohammed and Ali have applied to an **apprenticeship** program with a local construction company. They want to stay in Germany and have successful careers. I am studying hard at school. I hope I will be able to get place at university to study medicine.

Saja wants to wear clothes and makeup like her German friends. She has had many fights with Mama and Baba. She argues she should have the right to make her own decisions.

Sometimes I feel as though my memories of Syria are slipping away. I can hardly remember what our home looked like there. Mama and Baba still tell us stories of our lives in Aleppo. They encourage us to speak Arabic when we are together. But often it is easier for me to find the words in German.

This young Syrian refugee (right) is just beginning a training course with a German telephone company. His mentor, or adviser, is behind him.

Do Not Forget Our Stories!

Children around the world face huge challenges as refugees. Those living in refugee camps often have an uncertain future. Those in host countries may feel lonely. They may struggle to understand their new surroundings and ways of life.

Many Syrians are frustrated and sad. The fighting in their homeland seems to have no end in sight. They wonder if their country will ever see peace. Hundreds of thousands of people have died and millions have been forced to flee. While some refugees dream of returning to Syria one day, others want to start over in their new countries.

Refugees need help from others as they start new lives far from their families, friends, and homeland.

UN Rights of the Child

You have the right to live in freedom, with **dignity** and the promise of a bright future.

Refugees contribute in many ways to their new countries. They bring new ideas, values, and traditions. These create communities that have more variety. The stories of refugees can help people understand the problems they have faced. This can help build bridges between local people and refugee newcomers in host countries.

So many people are affected by violence around the world today. Often they do not make the headline news. But we should not forget their stories. As you hear their stories, think about ways that you can help refugees in your own community and around the world.

Discussion Prompts

1. What are some of the biggest challenges for refugees as they try to start new lives in Germany?
2. In what ways do refugees contribute to and enrich their communities?
3. Why do some people in Germany worry about the refugees in their country?

Glossary

apprenticeship An opportunity to learn a new job or skill by working for a fixed period of time with someone who is an expert in the field

asylum Protection given to refugees by a country

burqas Garments that cover the entire body, sometimes worn by Muslim women outside the home

carpenter Someone who makes and fixes wooden objects

civil war A war between groups of people in the same country

culture The shared beliefs, values, traditions, arts, and ways of life of a group of people

dignity Being worthy of respect

discrimination Unfair treatment of a person due to race, gender, or age

electrician Someone who works on electrical equipment

enrich To improve the quality

hijab A covering worn by Muslim women over the head and neck

host country A country that offers to give refugees a home

humanitarian crisis An event that brings harm to the health, safety, and well-being of a large group of people

immigrant Someone who voluntarily leaves one country to live in another

Middle East Countries in southwestern Asia and northern Africa that stretch from Libya to Afghanistan

mosque A Muslim place of worship

Muslim A follower of Islam

protested Demonstrated to show disapproval of something

racism The belief that some races of people are not equal to others

rebel groups People who fight against a country's government

refugees People who flee from their own country to another due to unsafe conditions

responsibility The duty to deal with something

rights Privileges and freedoms protected by law

smugglers People who move people or things illegally

temporary For a limited time

volunteers People who offer to work for no pay

Learning More

Books

Alabed, Bana. *Dear World: A Syrian Girls' Story of War and Plea for Peace.* Simon and Schuster, 2017.

Kullab, Samya. *Escape from Syria.* Firefly Books, 2017.

McCarney, Rosemary. *Where Will I Live?* Second Story Press, 2017.

Websites

www.iamsyria.org/why-should-we-help-syrian-refugees.html
Watch this short video to hear about why young people around the world think everyone should help refugees.

www.unhcr.ca/wp-content/uploads/2014/10/poetry_book.pdf
Take a look at this collection of poems written by young people in recognition of World Refugee Day.

www.unicef.org/rightsite/files/uncrcchilldfriendlylanguage.pdf
Explore the United Nations Convention on the Rights of the Child.

Index

About the Author

Linda Barghoorn studied languages in university because she wanted to travel the world. She has visited 60 countries, taking photographs and writing stories about the people and cultures of our planet. At home, she volunteers at a local agency that provides newcomers and their families with clothing and community support.